SPEED PICKING

by FRANK GAMBALE

DEDICATION

I would like to thank my family, Mom and Dad, Nunz, Sav, Maureen, Laurence and Paul for all the love and support. To Iain Scott for the idea to write a book and to all the staff at G.I.T. (Guitar Institute of Technology)

Thanks Mates

PLAYBACK+
Speed • Pitch • Balance • Loop

To access audio online, visit:
www.halleonard.com/mylibrary
Enter Code
1503-4397-1842-9553

Cover Photo by William Hames

ISBN 978-0-7935-2751-9

HAL•LEONARD®
7777 W. BLUEMOUND RD. P.O. BOX 13819 MILWAUKEE, WI 53213

Copyright © 1985, 1994 by HAL LEONARD CORPORATION
International Copyright Secured   All Rights Reserved

For all works contained herein:
Unauthorized copying, arranging, adapting, recording, Internet posting, public performance,
or other distribution of the printed or recorded music in this publication is an infringement of copyright.
Infringers are liable under the law.

Visit Hal Leonard Online at
www.halleonard.com

Speed Picking

Over the years of playing, performing and teaching guitar, one of the biggest problems encountered is not with the left hand fingerings as much as with the right hand picking technique. Many guitarists openly admit that their picking is pretty bad.

Unfortunately, there is not much written on this particular subject and that is the purpose of this book, to give you an insight into the techniques that I have been developing and using that really work. The basic idea has been with us for many years and can be used to achieve mind-boggling speed and flawless accuracy while being completely relaxed in the right hand.

I refer to this style of picking as SPEED PICKING (sometimes referred to as sweep picking). A lot of us know at least one SPEED PICKING lick:

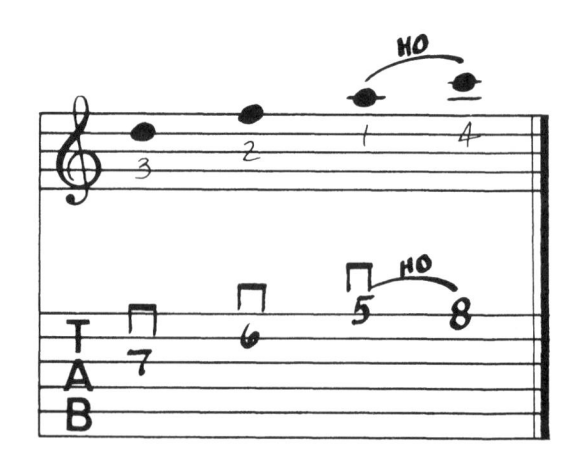

Example #1

In this example of SPEED PICKING, one down stroke is used for the first 3 notes and a Hammer-on for the last note. Most guitarists have played this simple lick at some time or another and leave the technique at that, little knowing how far this germ of an idea may be taken.

The most common style of picking today is 'Alternate' picking (down up down) or the reverse (up down up) which is an excellent way to pick and I am by no means trying to talk anyone out of it. What I am trying to do is broaden your horizon. Alternate picking is fine for scale-type runs but just doesn't cut it for arpeggios or lines where there is only one note per string for example.

SPEED PICKING is actually partly alternate picking except, whenever a string is crossed, one stroke is used for the two notes whether going from low to high or the reverse.

Example #2

So as you can see in example #2, each time you change string, a single down stroke is used in each case. So, this is the most fundamental pattern for this picking approach (down up down down up down down up etc).

Another important thing is the use of scale patterns with three (3) notes per string. SPEED PICKING lends itself to these, but be sure that when you practice these patterns to keep the notes 8th's or 16th's. Because of the three note system it's easy to play everything as triplets. Also, there is a tendancy at first to accent the first note of every string, like accenting the first note of every triplet. This situation is normal and just takes a little time to get used to the feeling of using a single stroke when crossing strings. You can see almost immediately that the amount of right hand picking is reduced by 1/3, a lot less work required to play the same amount of notes.

Now that you've played the scale from low to high, you're probably wondering how to get back down. Conveniently, the last notes in example #2 on the first string were played with a down then an up stroke, so we can go directly back to the second string and continue with the picking strokes in reverse. Also, note that there are only two notes on the 1st string.

Example #3

So basically, when picking a scale from low to high, it is DOWN UP DOWN DOWN UP etc., and from high to low it is UP DOWN UP UP DOWN etc. Notice that when picking in one direction either low to high or high to low, the number of notes per string is odd (1, 3 or 5). When a change of direction is needed, an even number of notes on a string is required (2 or 4). As you can see when you played the scale there were 3 notes per string (odd) until the 1st string, then there was 2 notes on the 1st string (even) to change direction then back to 3 notes per string (odd) until the 6th string where there was 4 notes (even) to change direction.

<u>WARNING</u>: This technique will feel awkward for a while until you get the hang of it, but believe me it's well worth the effort. It reduces the amount of picking required to play, and the beauty of it is, as you will see after going through this book, is that it works equally well for scales, arpeggios, licks etc.

Examples 2 and 3 are designed to give you the idea of going up the scale then connecting it to come back down, so here we have some more examples of scales and related modes;

Example #4

Here are two short exercises to strengthen the UP stroke (example #5) and both the UP and DOWN strokes in example #6.

Example #5

Example #6

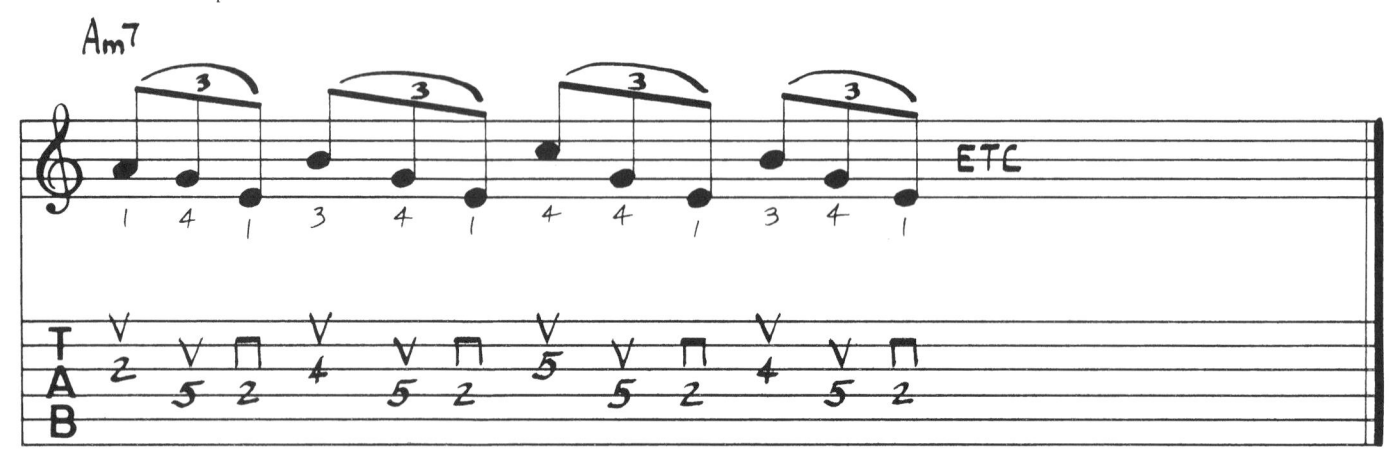

Remember to keep all the notes separate, like playing stacatto. I suggest that to begin with, the Major scales and related modes (Dorian, Phrygian, Lydian etc) be played three (3) notes per string with two (2) notes on the 1st string enabling you to reverse the picking direction to come back down, then four (4) notes on the 6th string. This pattern is 4 bars of 8th notes or 2 bars of 16th notes. So the scales and modes will look like this:

Example #7　　　　　　　　　　(G Major scale)

Position 2, Dorian scale has already been given in example #4. Simply transpose it down a whole step to the key of G and begin on A.

Example #8　　　　　　　　　　(B Phrygian Mode)

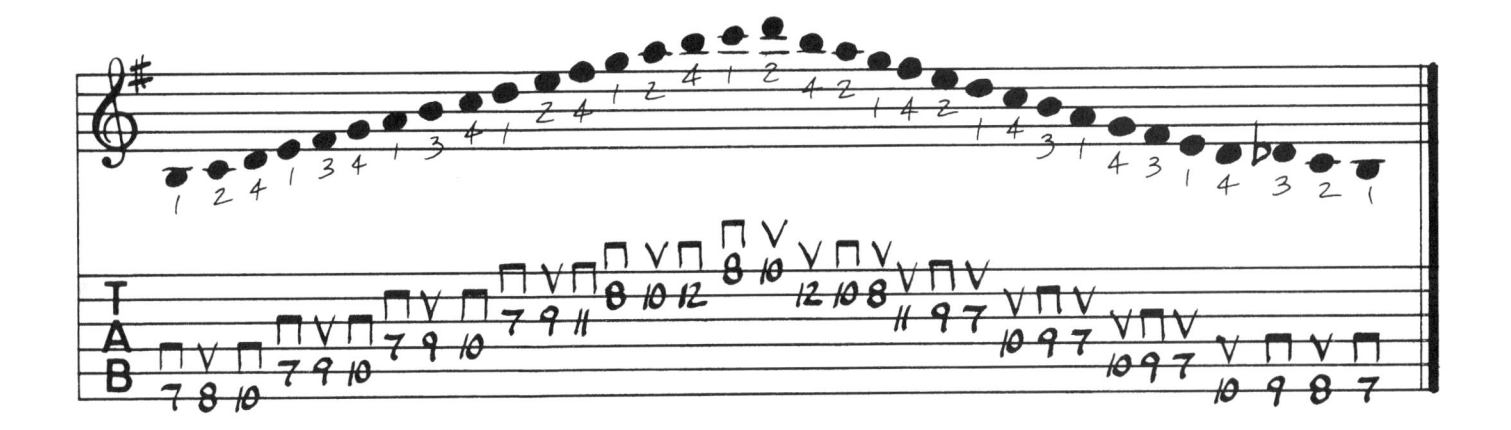

The best thing about playing your scales with this three (3) note per string idea is that every scale only has one (1) picking pattern. So, the right hand comes together very quickly! There's no need to change your picking as required for traditional scale patterns.

These scales take a bit of stretching as they can cover a great deal of the fingerboard. SPEED PICKING is the only way you'll find to play some of the faster lines played by saxophone or keyboard players. This approach for me came from necessity (the mother of invention) so that I could emulate those instruments. You'll find later on in this book that some of the lines are unguitaristic but once you have them down they sound terrific on guitar.

By now I think you get the idea with the straight scale forms. Don't forget that you can use the same three (3) note scale concept for other scales like the Melodic minor and the Diminished scales. Now let's look at some scale sequences;

Example #9

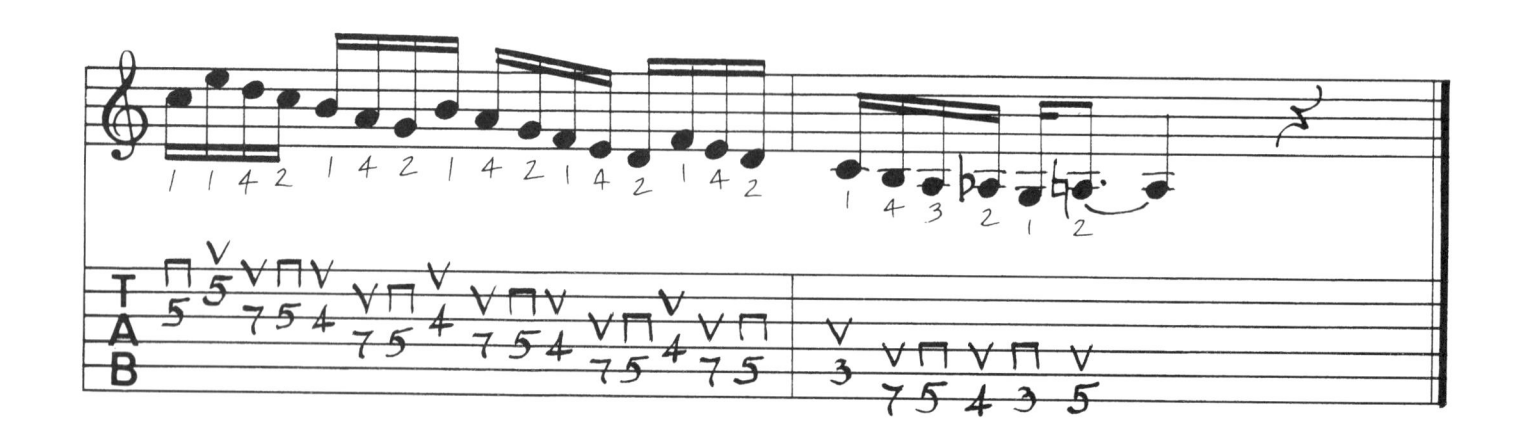

Practice example #9 slowly, then build up speed gradually. Remember to keep each note separate, especially when crossing strings.

This exercise incorporates triads.

Example #10

Here's another way of approaching the SPEED PICKING technique. We have three (3) notes on a string, one (1) note on the following string, then three (3) notes on the next string etc. Here's an example:

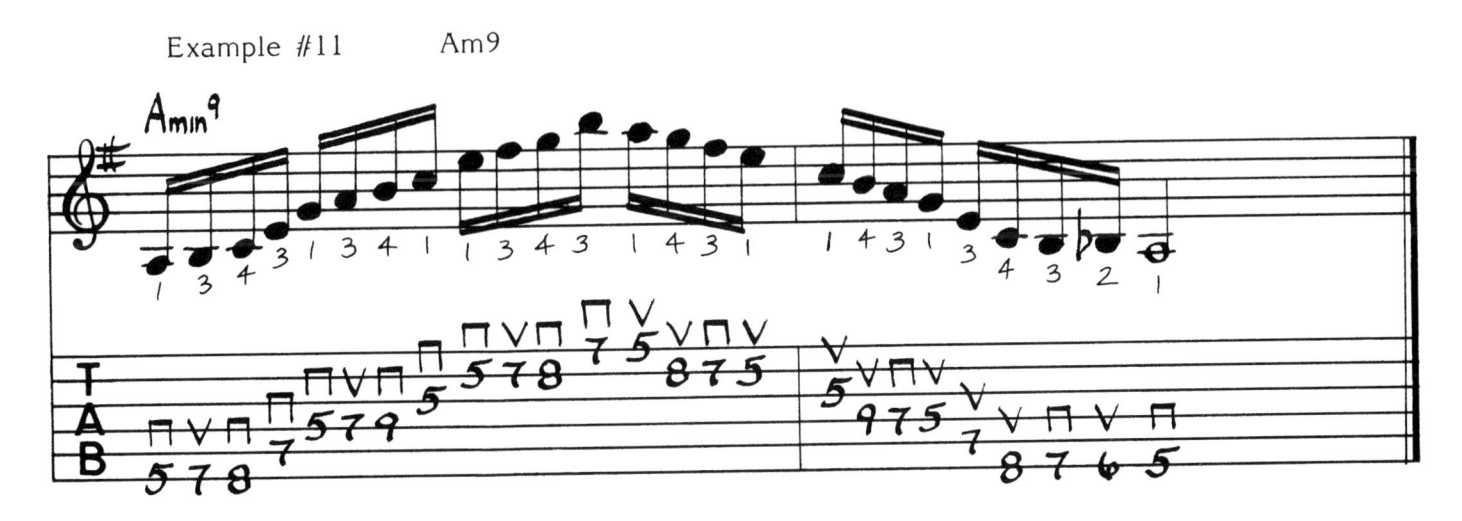

Example #11   Am9

The example above uses all of the picking crossovers used so far: two (2) or three (3) down strokes, depending on whether you cross 2 or 3 strings, 1 or 3 notes on a string going in one direction either up or down, 2 notes on a string to change direction, then up strokes crossing strings on the way down, then 4 notes on the 6th string to return us to the beginning stroke.

By now you should be recognizing some picking patterns and understanding the logic behind it. You can see that it is a powerful tool. It is the economy of picking motion. The less you have to move the pick up and down, the more you will naturally increase your speed to play lines that seemed impossible or unguitaristic. But we're only scratching the surface so let's continue.

Pentatonic Scales and Speed Picking

Let's now apply all you've learned so far to some Pentatonic scales. I'll warn you now that these fingerings are probably somewhat different to what you're used to. Once again they require you to stretch about 6 frets or more, the results are well worth it though.

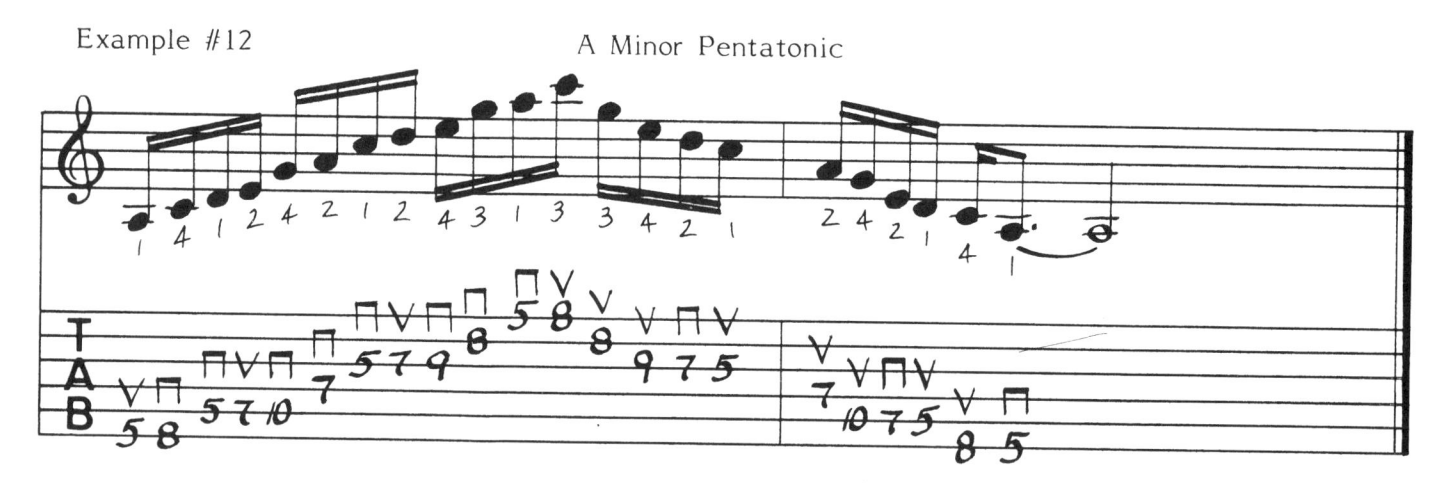

Example #12 — A Minor Pentatonic

The next position for A Minor Pentatonic looks like this:

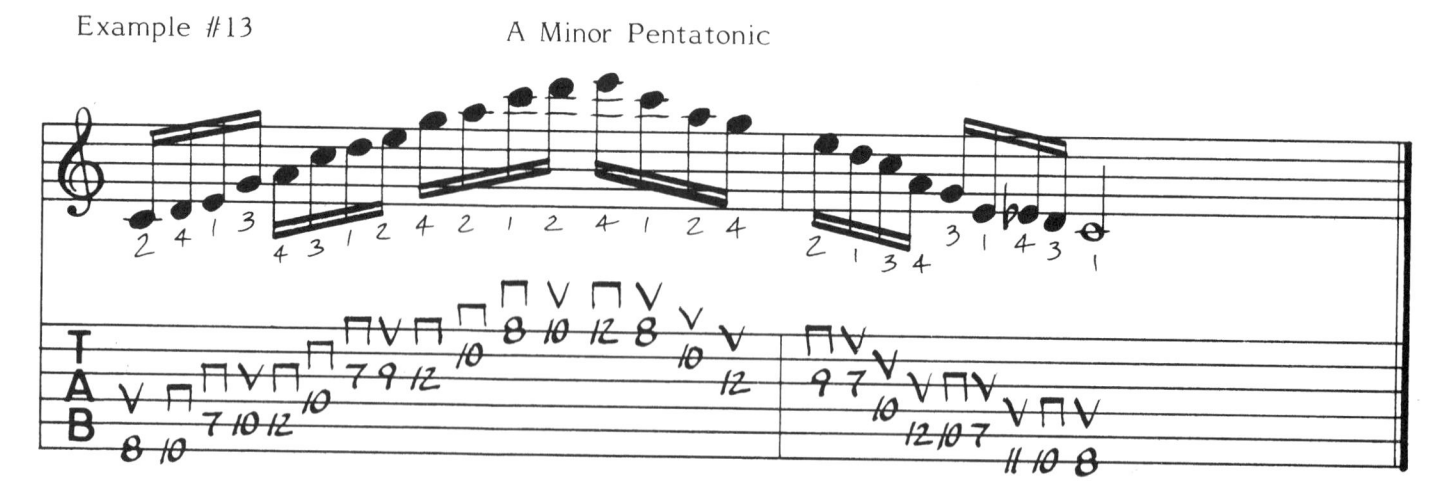

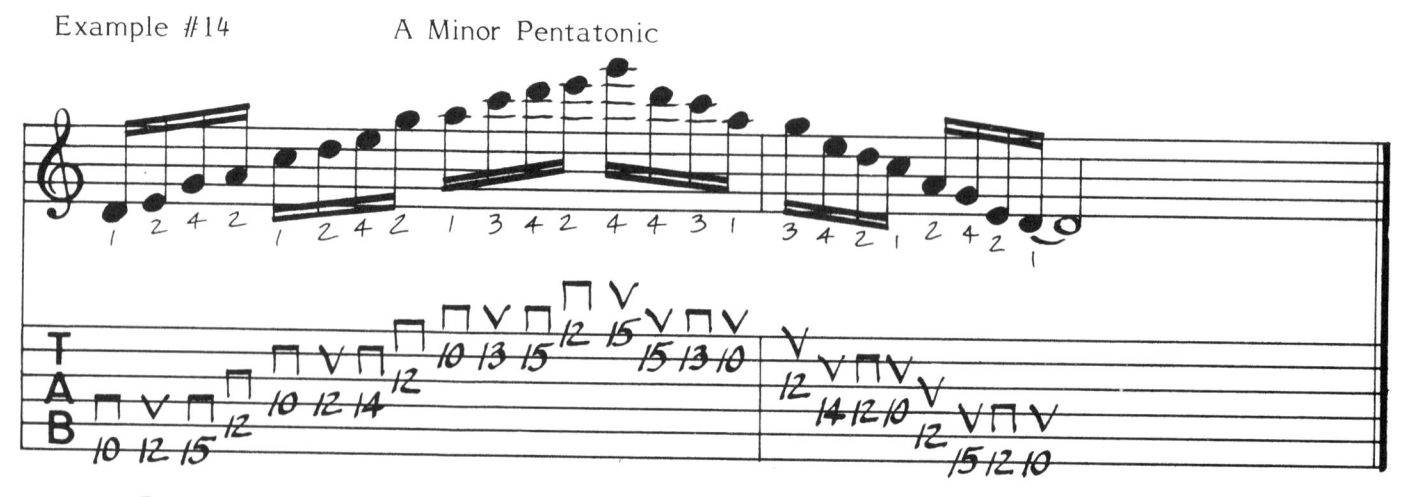

Example #13 — A Minor Pentatonic

Example #14 — A Minor Pentatonic

Remember, with these ideas, you don't have to play the whole scale. If there's a section of it that grabs you, take it out, mess with it, and create your own ideas from it.

Pentatonic Supplement

Here's a few Pentatonic ideas.

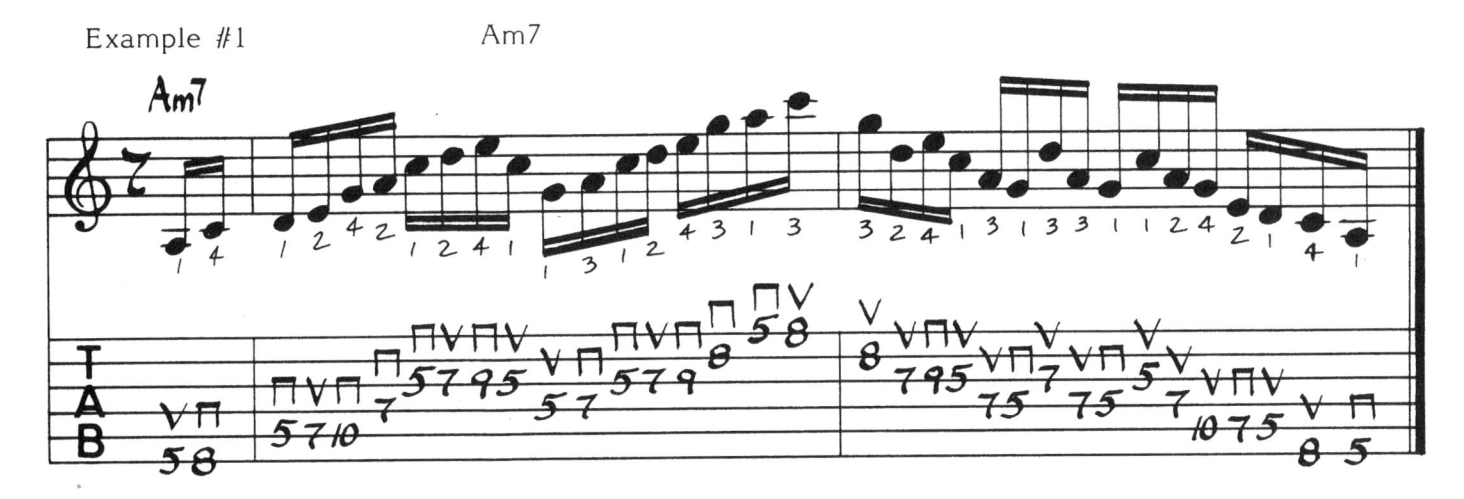

Example #1

These examples will work well over any of the following chords: Am7, Am9, Am11, Fmaj7, Fmaj9, C/D, D11, F#7#5b9, F#7#5#9, F#7b9 etc, Gm7, Gm9, Gm11, C/Bb, Bbmaj7, Bbmaj7#11 etc.

Example #2

This next example is a very important one. It lays out some concepts of interconnecting patterns. It moves around the fretboard a fair bit, and it's a lot of fun to master.

Example #3

This one is a very common Pentatonic pattern ala Jean-luc Ponty. The notes are orthodox but the way it is played is unorthodox.

Example #4

The next one is a cycle pattern which can be used for building intensity in a solo. It has a ten (10) note repeating phrase then leaps out at the end. This is a saxophone-type lick.

Example #5

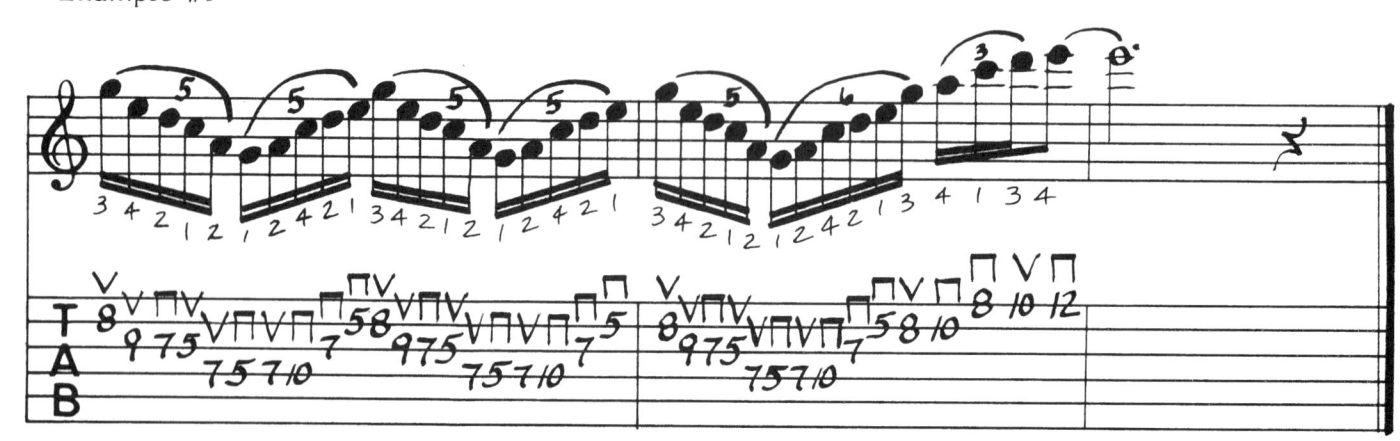

Arpeggios and Speed Picking

A lot of the arpeggios you'll encounter in this section use picking patterns already learned, namely, one note on two adjoining strings (E and A), then three notes on the next string (D) etc.

Example #15   Cmaj7 arpeggio

Cmaj7 arpeggio, two octaves in a different position. This one requires some hand movement.

Example #16

One more Cmaj7 arpeggio.

Example #17

Meeting with Major Sevenths

In this piece of music, only Cmaj7 and Dbmaj7 arpeggios are used. Cmaj7 is equal to Am9, Fmaj9#11, so I have harmonized this piece with diatonic (from the major scale) chords, so you see, one major 7 arpeggio can be used over many different chords. This type of information is very important to remember because it reduces the amount of learning needed, and can make playing changes considerably easier.

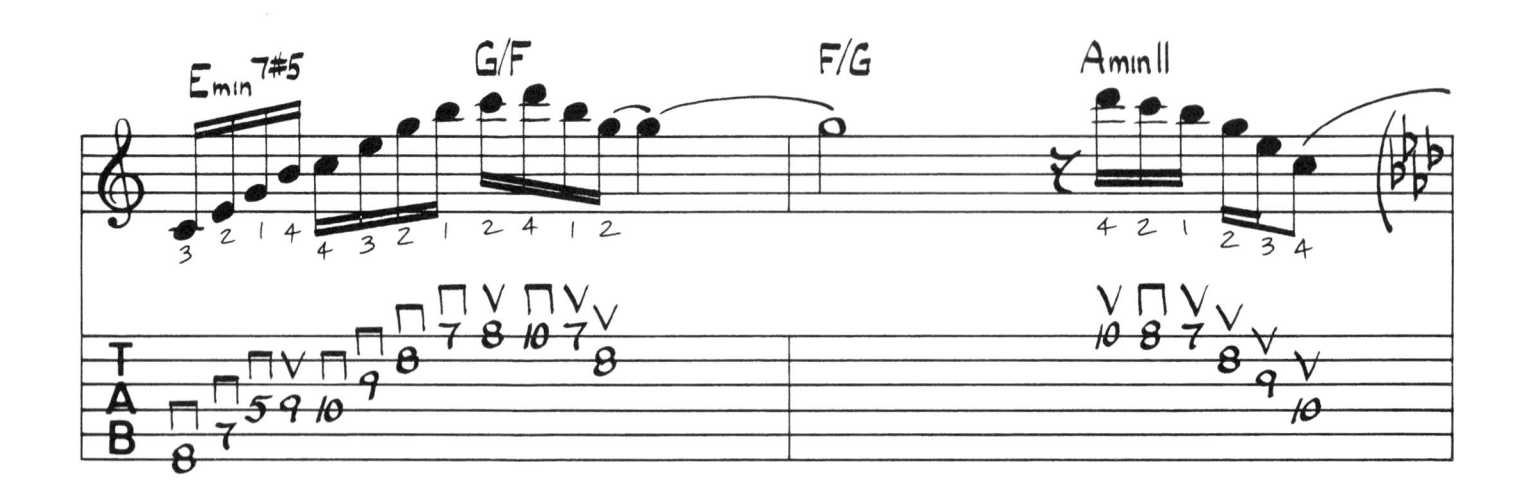

12

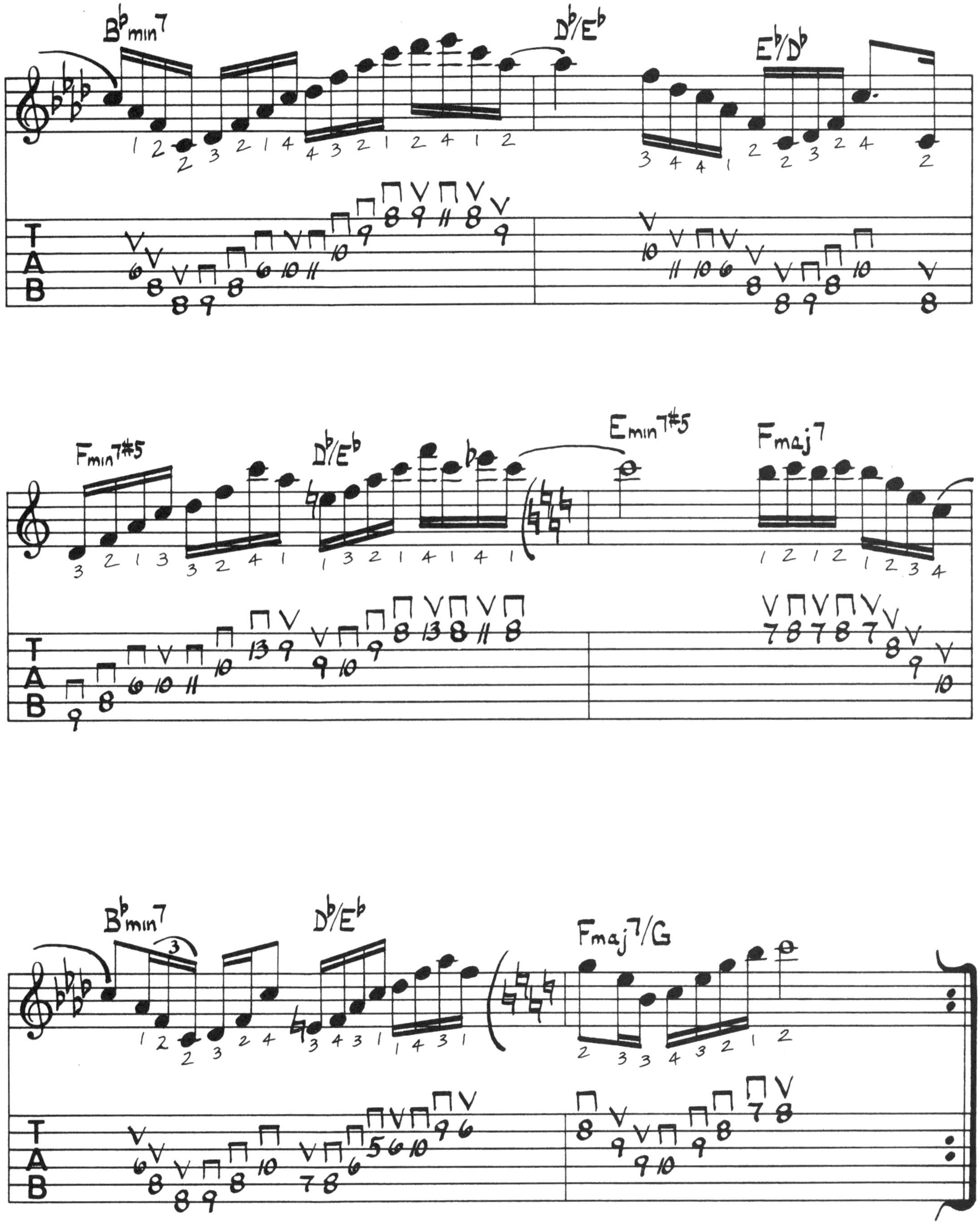
B♭min7
D♭/E♭
E♭/D♭
Fmin7#5
D♭/E♭
Emin7#5
Fmaj7
B♭min7
D♭/E♭
Fmaj7/G
TAB

Here's a minor 7th arpeggio with the same picking pattern as the major 7th arpeggio.

Example #18

An important point to remember is to see the chord shape when you play these arpeggios. All an arpeggio is, is a chord broken up and played with the individual notes. So, in the example above, on strings 4, 3, 2 and 1, it is simply the shape of a Cm7 chord voicing 1, b3, 5, b7, and the shape of a straight C minor descending. So don't forget the chord shapes while soloing with SPEED PICKING.

You can also use all the diatonic scale arpeggios over a static (non-moving) chord. For example, try using all the arpeggios of C major (Cmaj7, Dm7, Em7, Fmaj7, G7, Am7, Bm7b5) all over a Dm7 chord. The notes of Cm7 are also the notes of Eb6, Abmaj9 (without the root), F11, Eb/F (no root), so once again, one arpeggio can have many applications.

Yet another Cm7 arpeggio.

Example #19

Let's say that you want to play extensions on these shapes e.g., maj9, min9, dom9, just add the 9th's to familiar arpeggio shapes like the following exercises;

Example #20   Cmaj9 arpeggio

Example #21   Cm11 arpeggio

I wish to emphasize and repeat that these arpeggios are interchangeable, i.e., Ebmaj7 = Cm9, Cm7 = Eb6, Cm11 = Ebmaj9, try to think of as many applications as possible for one shape, one arpeggio can go a long way.

Example #22   C9 arpeggio

Example #23

Another C9 arpeggio shape.

Exercise #23 is a difficult one to execute cleanly, what I suggest here, as with all the exercises in this section, try not to keep your left hand in one fixed position, try to leave it free to move over the 6 or so frets, poised, ready for the notes required. Don't try to stretch these unless you have unusually large hands and are capable of making this stretch with little effort. Be sure to keep all the notes separate and clean and as I said, move the poised hand position.

Now we'll look at a couple of altered arpeggios.

Example #24   C7#5#9 arpeggio

These altered arpeggios are not completely strict in the sense that they do not always include the notes from the chord in each octave, though they do capture the required notes over the entirety of the exercise.

16

Example #25   C7#5b9 (same as DbmMaj7 arpeggio)

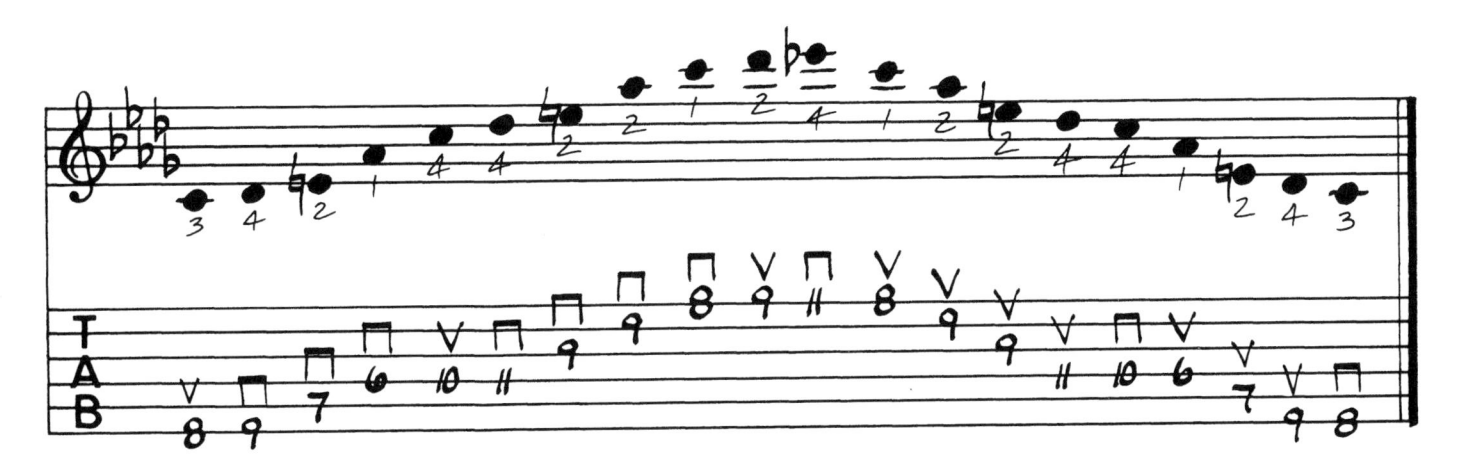

Triad Arpeggios and Speed Picking

Now at this point we'll look at some straight ahead Major and Minor arpeggios. I have left them until this point because they are the most difficult to play. Triad playing is very important in 80's music, because of the abundant use of slash chords i.e., triad chords with different bass notes, e.g., Bb/C, this chord creates a C11 sound although it is not, technically speaking, because of the absense of the 3rd and 5th from C major. Bb/C is a voicing of its own, having its own sound. If we analyze this voicing, it is a Bb triad, Notes Bb, D and F, which is the b7, 9 and 11 of C major, plus of course the C root.

This is just one possibility of a slash chord, all combinations have been used, and all are very much a part of modern music. Getting back to the arpeggios, when you play a atraight A major (1 3 5) arpeggio over an A/B chord, it's very "hip" sounding and certainly doesn't sound like a regular 1, 3, 5 triad.

Here are the other possibilities of slash chords using an A major triad from inside to the most outside sounding ones.

1. A/B   (usually a V chord in E major)
2. A/D   (Dmaj9 sound without the 3rd, I or IV chord)
3. A/F#   (same as F#m7)
4. A/C#   (like a C#m7#5, III or VI chord)
5. A/E   (popular suspension chord)
6. A/G   (same as G6/9#11 or A7 with 7th in bass, IV chord)
7. A/F   (same as Fmaj7#5, III chord of D Melodic minor)
8. A/G#   (like an Amaj7 with the 7th in bass, III chord of E major)
9. A/Bb   (A chord with b9 in bass, Diminished Half-Whole from the A root)
10. A/C   (like C13b9 less b7, Diminished Half-Whole of C)
11. A/Eb (like an A7b5b9 less the 3rd)

Example #26   A major arpeggio

Example #27   This one covers a lot of territory very quickly.

Example #28   D major arpeggio

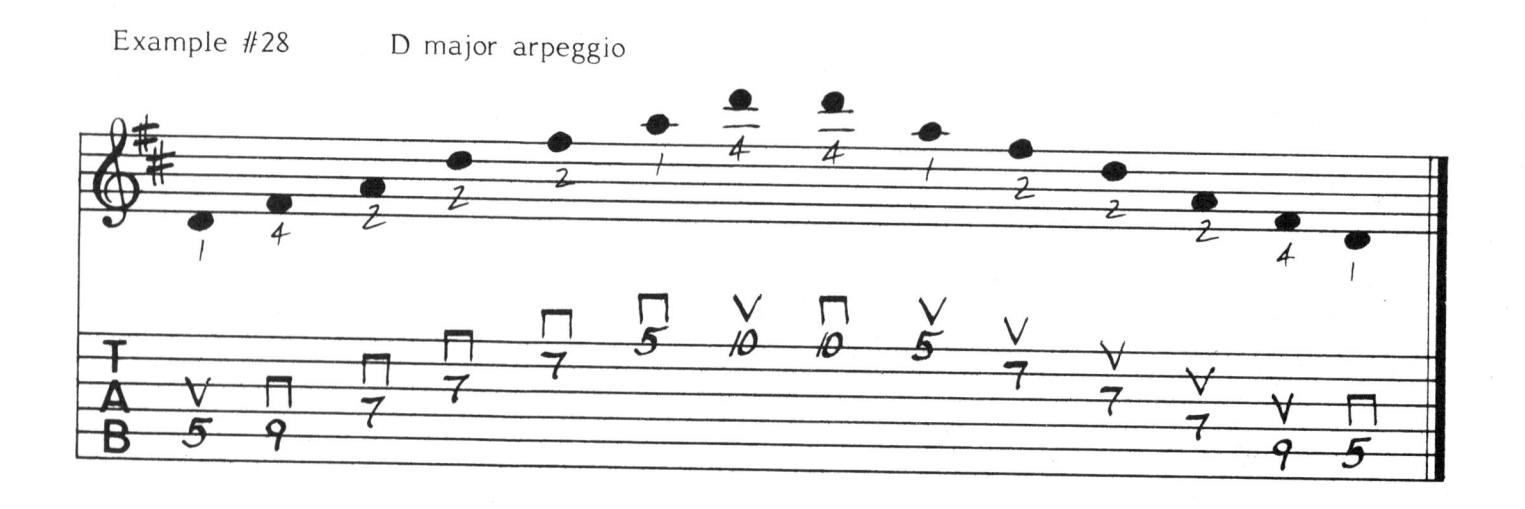

18

Example #29   F major arpeggio

Example #30   D minor arpeggio

Example #31   A minor arpeggio

Example #32   E major arpeggio

Example #33   E suspended 4 arpeggio

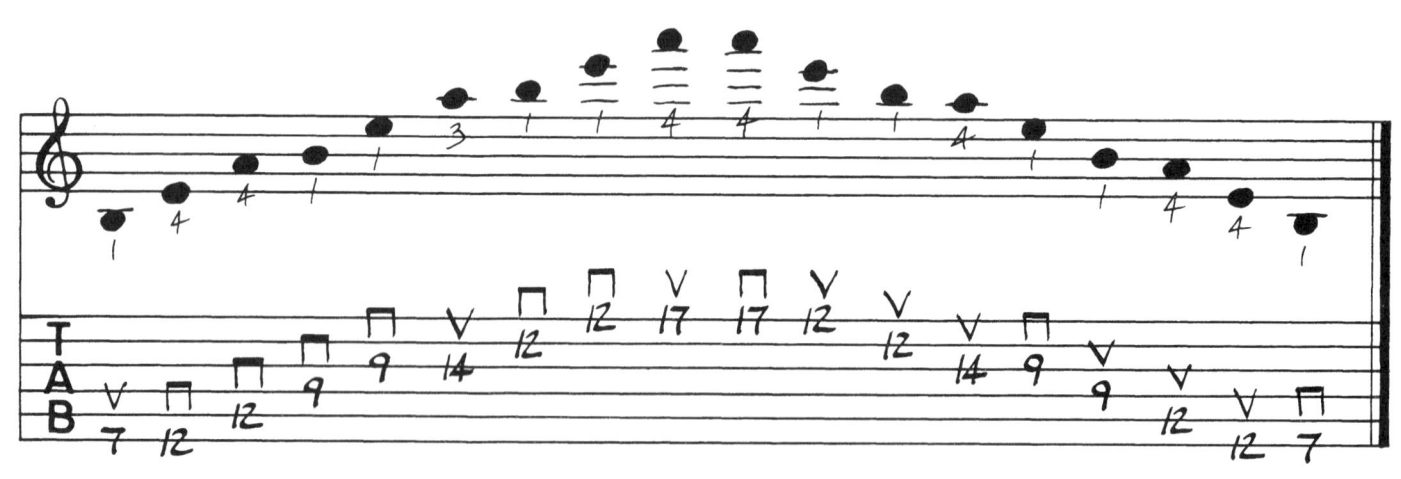

Example #34   F sus 4 arpeggio (somewhat easier than the last)

Example #35   C augmented (could be used over Bb13 or E7#9)

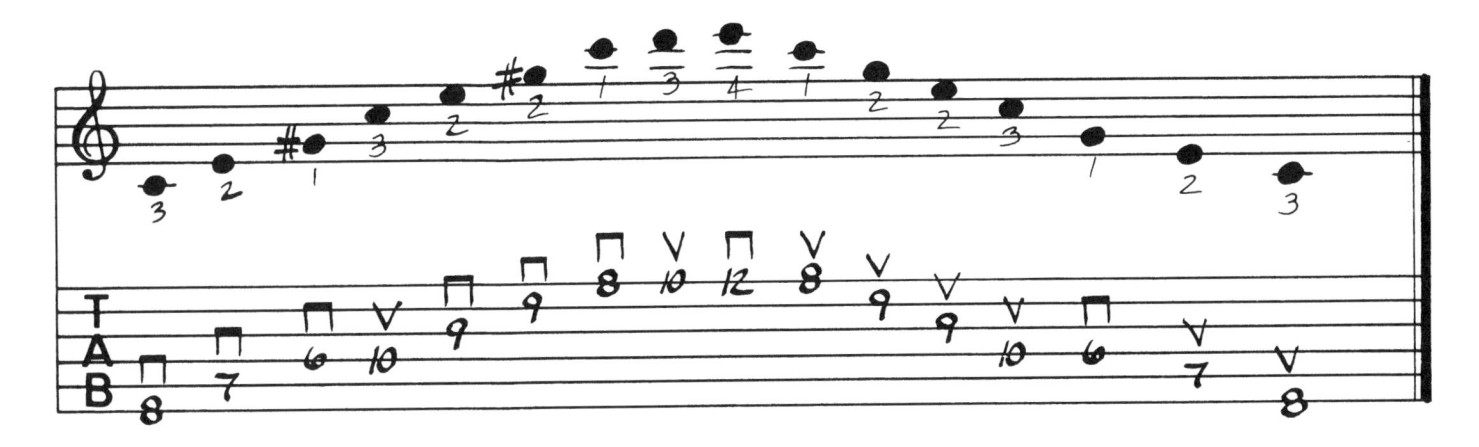

Don't forget, you can play these exercises without cross picking by using three (3) notes on the D and only two (2) notes or four (4) on the 1st string i.e., add a Bb note on the D string.

Example #36   C Diminished arpeggio (B7b9)

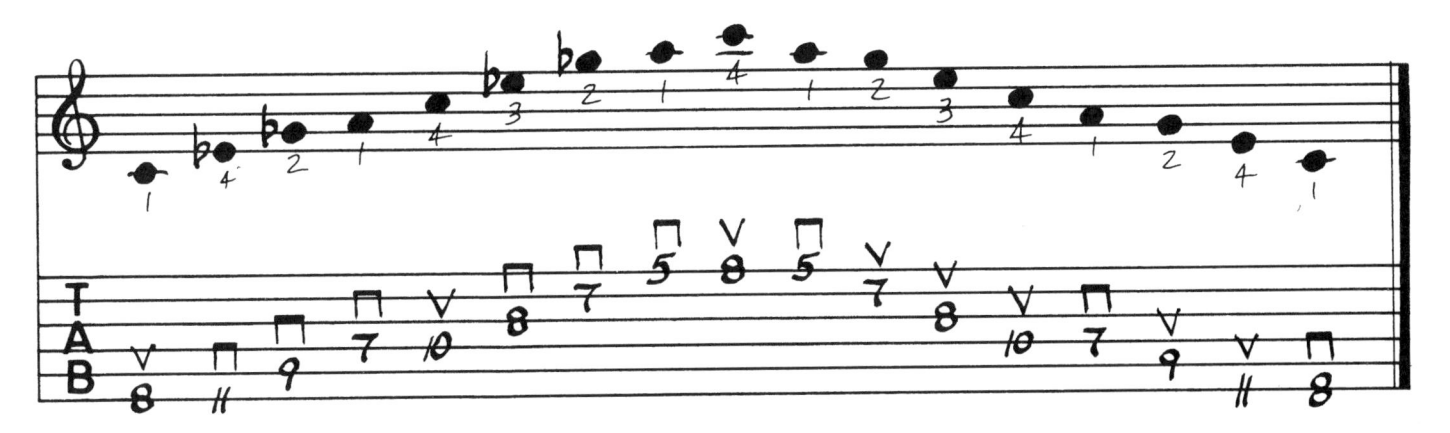

Triads and You

Note that in this piece I have used different harmonization for the same arpeggios i.e., in bar 1, the arpeggio is E major and the chord is also E major. In bar 2 however, the arpeggio is D major but the chord is Bm7. Feel free to reharmonize this piece remembering that you can use 12 different slash chord possibilities for every bar that is a straight major triad (nearly every bar).

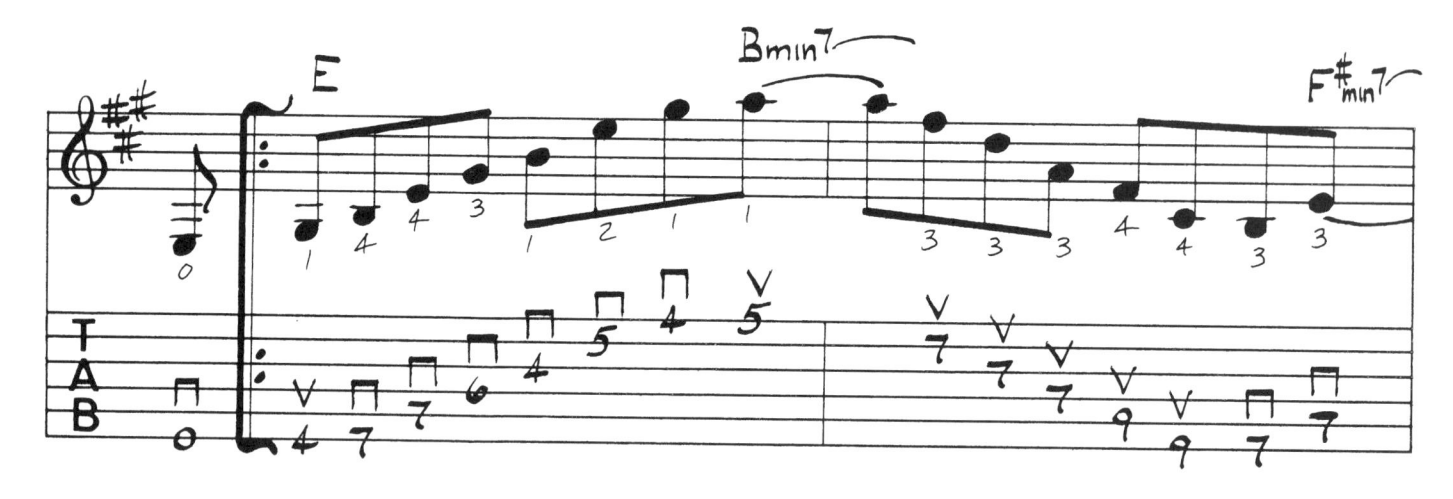

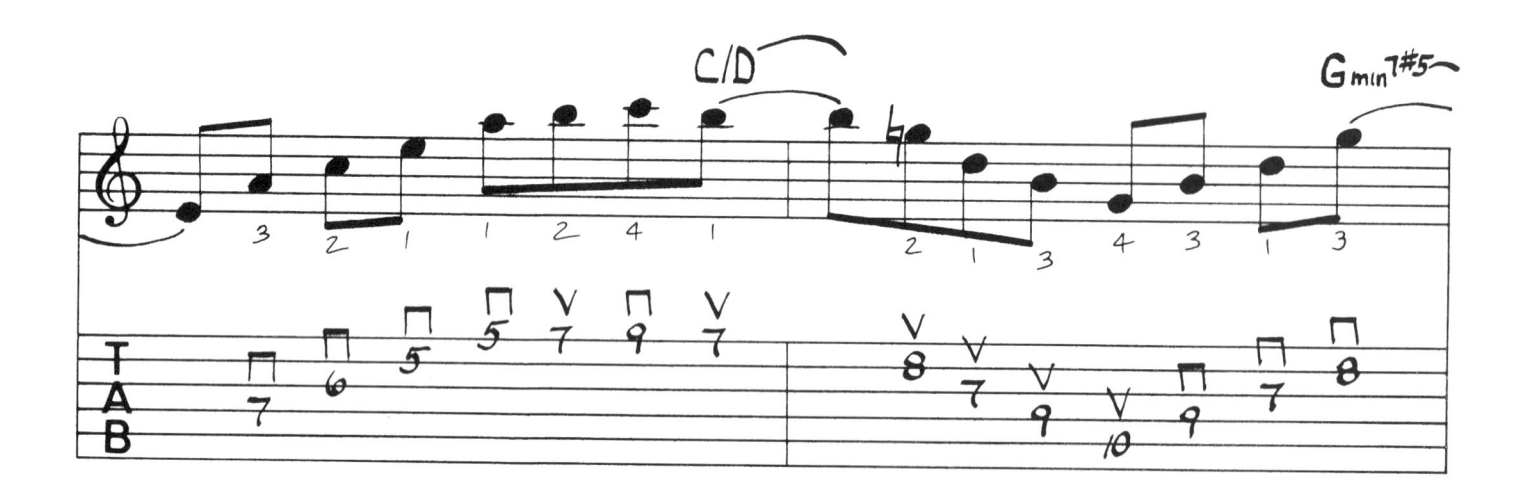

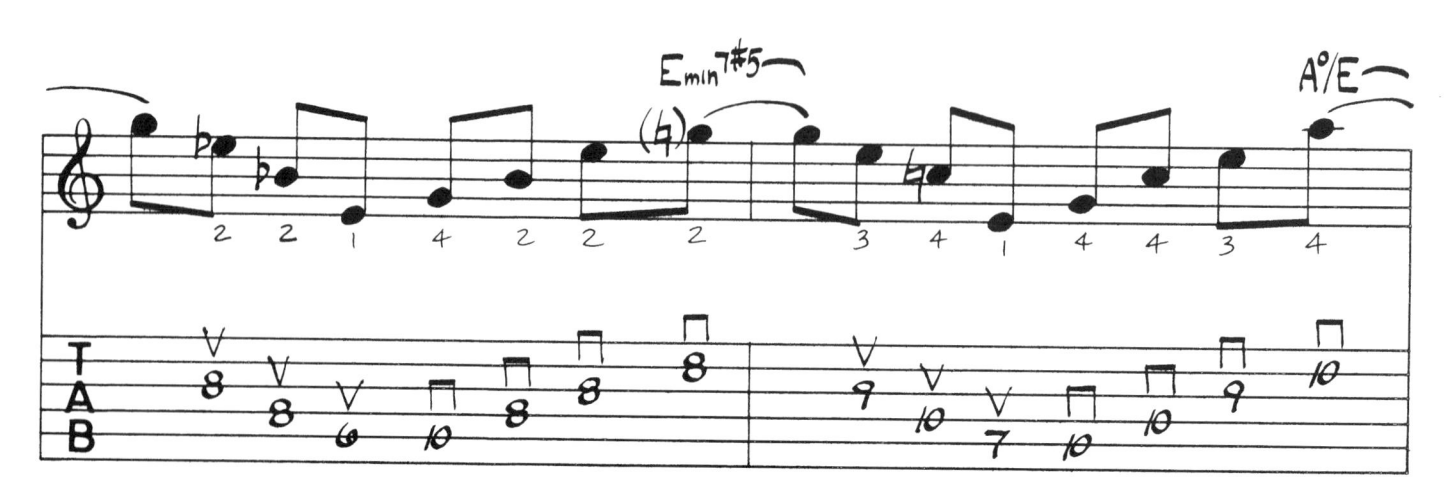

Triads and You (cont'd)

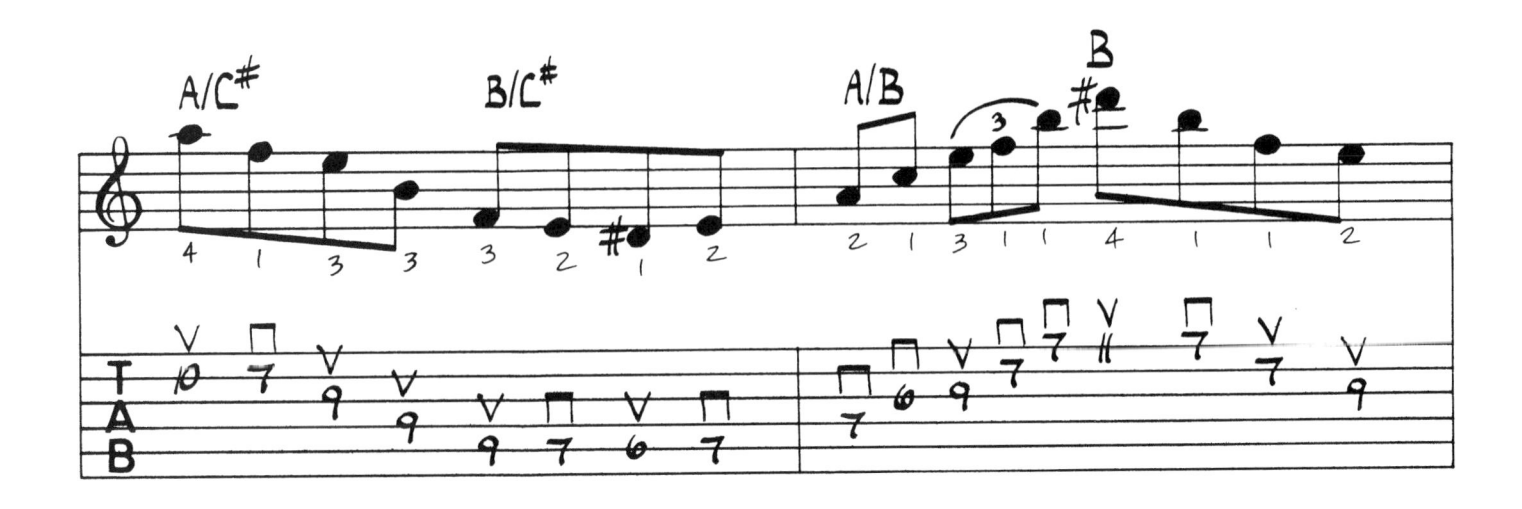

Speed Picking Licks

Lick #1   Am7 or C/D (D11) or Em7#5

Lick #2   Am7 or C/D (D11) or Em7#5

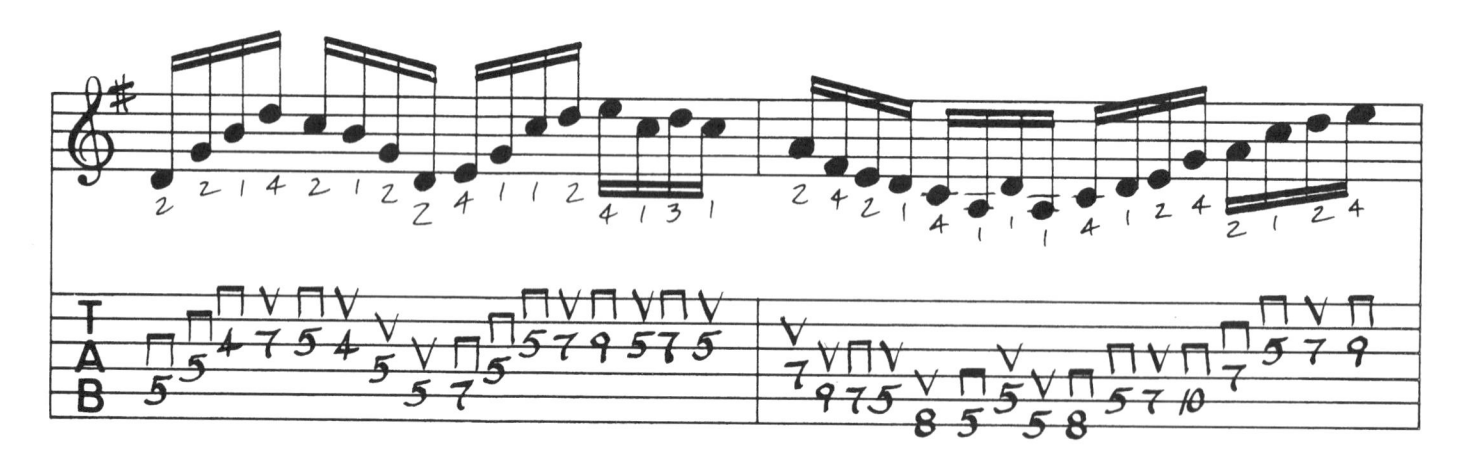

Lick #3 Dm7 or Fmaj7 or F/G

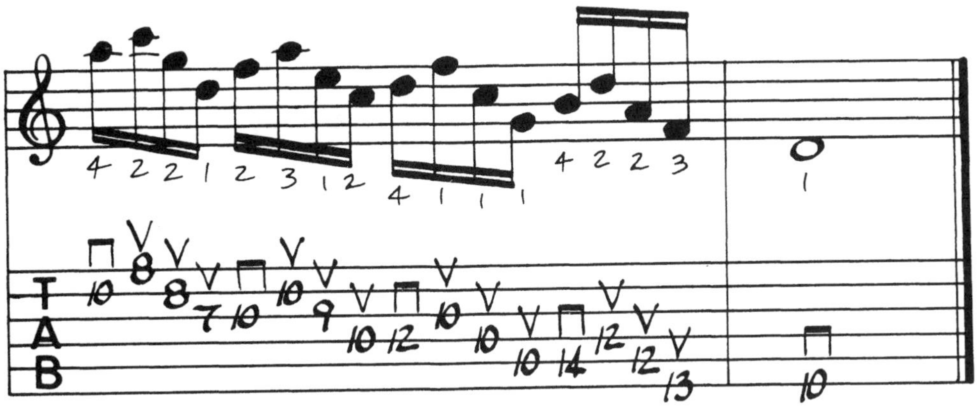

Lick #4 Am7 or C/D (D11)

Lick #5 Am7, D7#9, Gmaj7 (II V I)

Lick #6   Em7, A7#5, Dm7

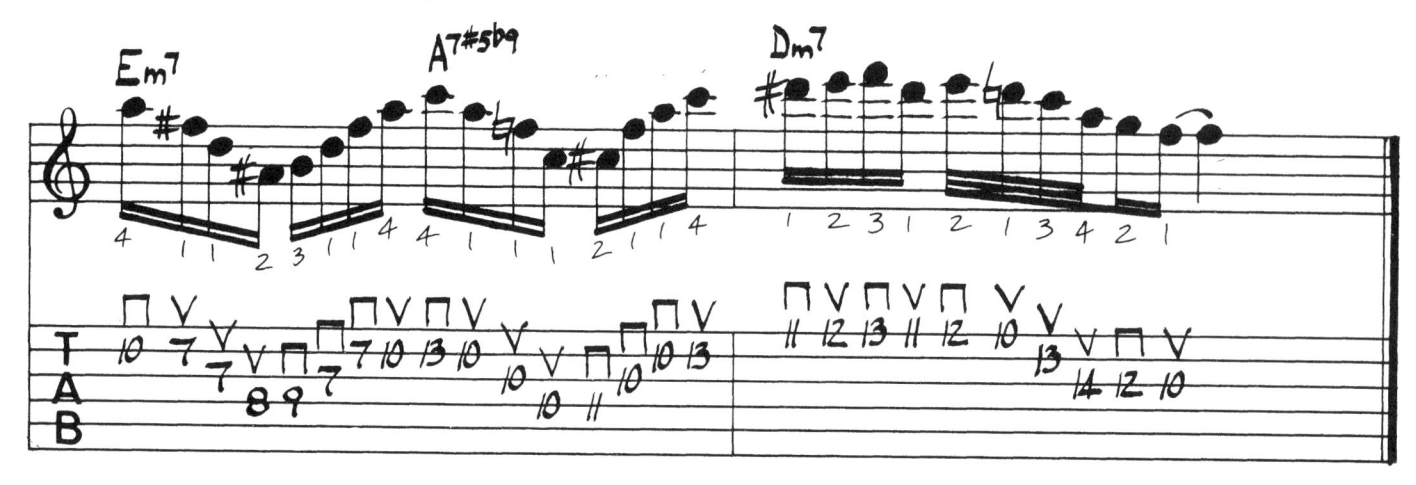

Lick #7   Em7, A7#5#9, Dm7

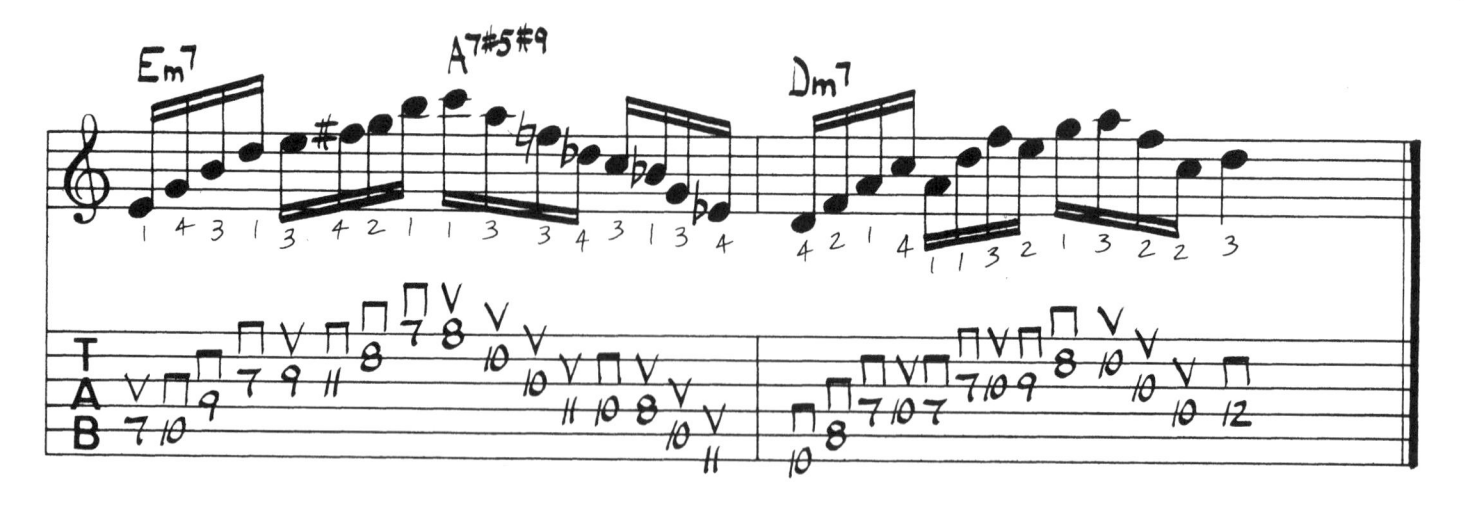

Lick #8   Em7b5, A7#5#9, Dm7

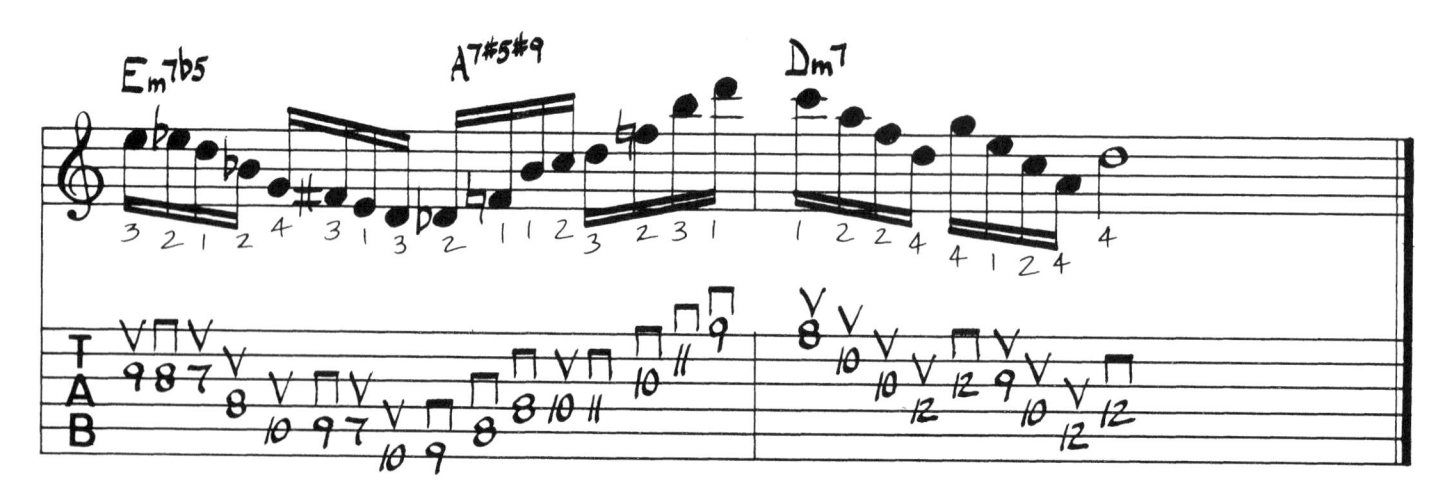

Lick #9   Em7, A7#5#9, Dmaj7

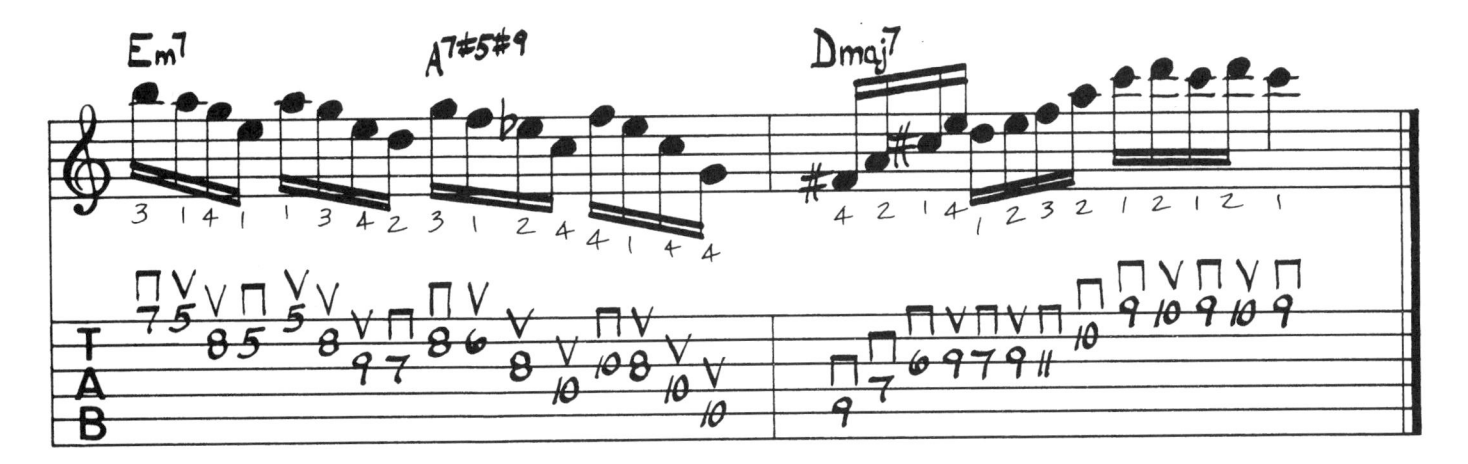

The fingerings for these examples are optional. I use them and they work for me. I suggest trying to use them because they facilitate the position changes.

Exercise #10 incorporates a scale type sequence idea that builds throughout the line. This line sounds great at high speed.

Lick #10

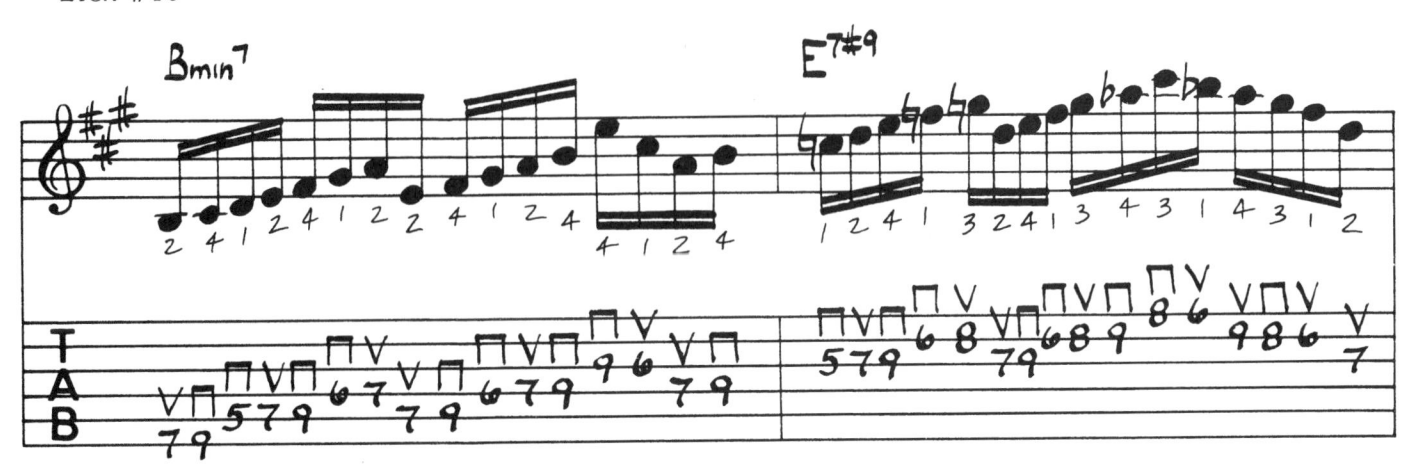

Lick #11   Bm7b5, E7#9, Am7

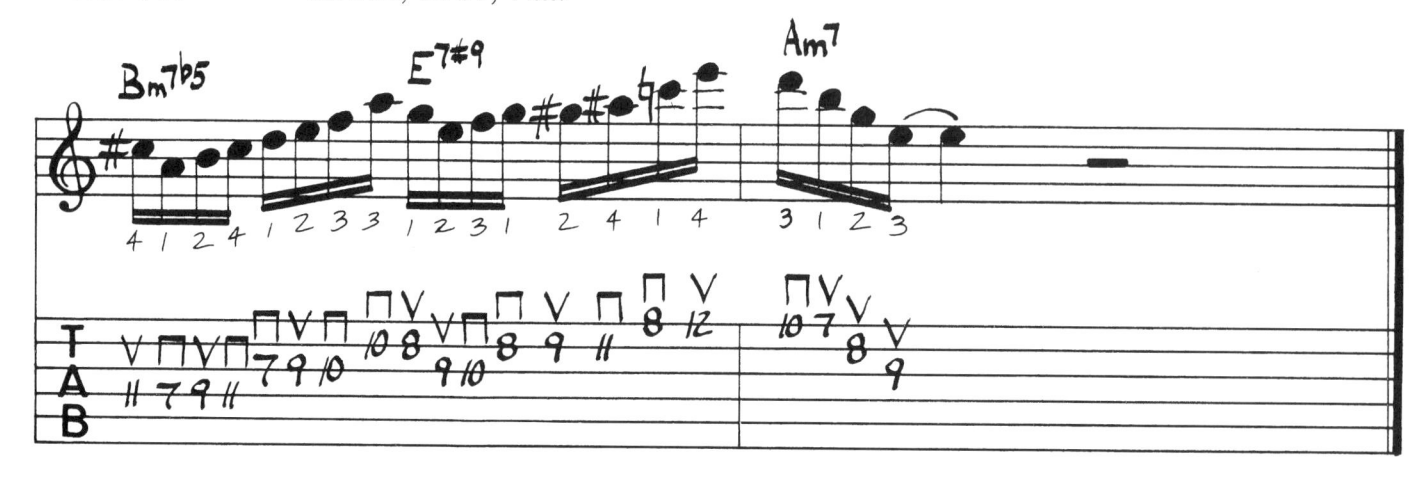

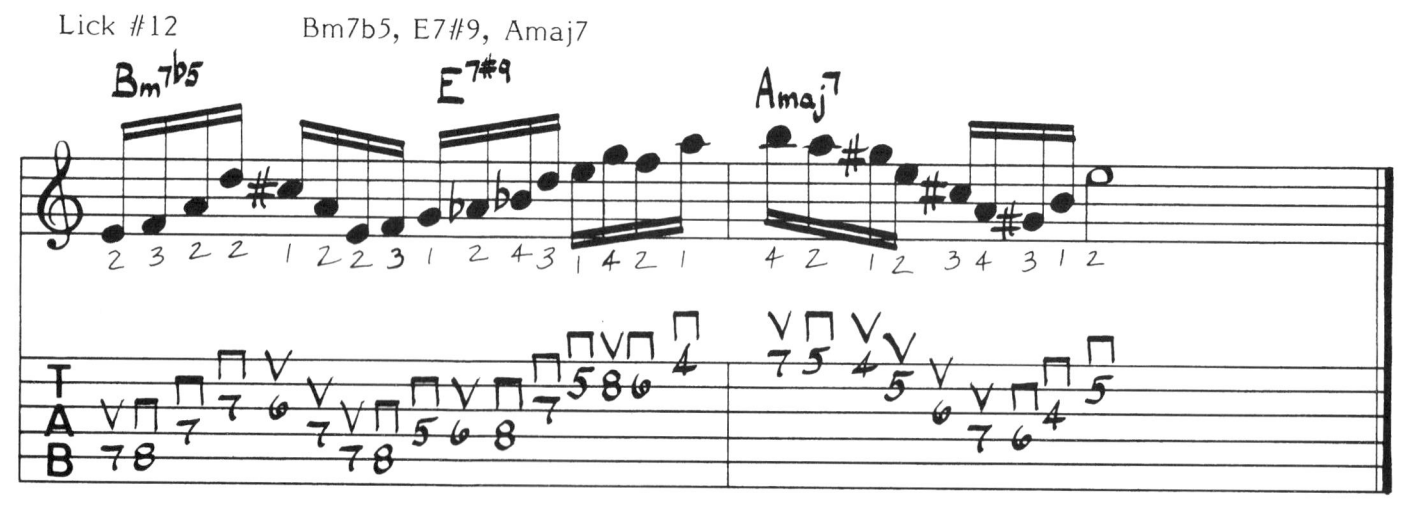

Lick #12   Bm7b5, E7#9, Amaj7

Lick #13   E9 or Bb7#5b9

Lick #14   G/A or Em7

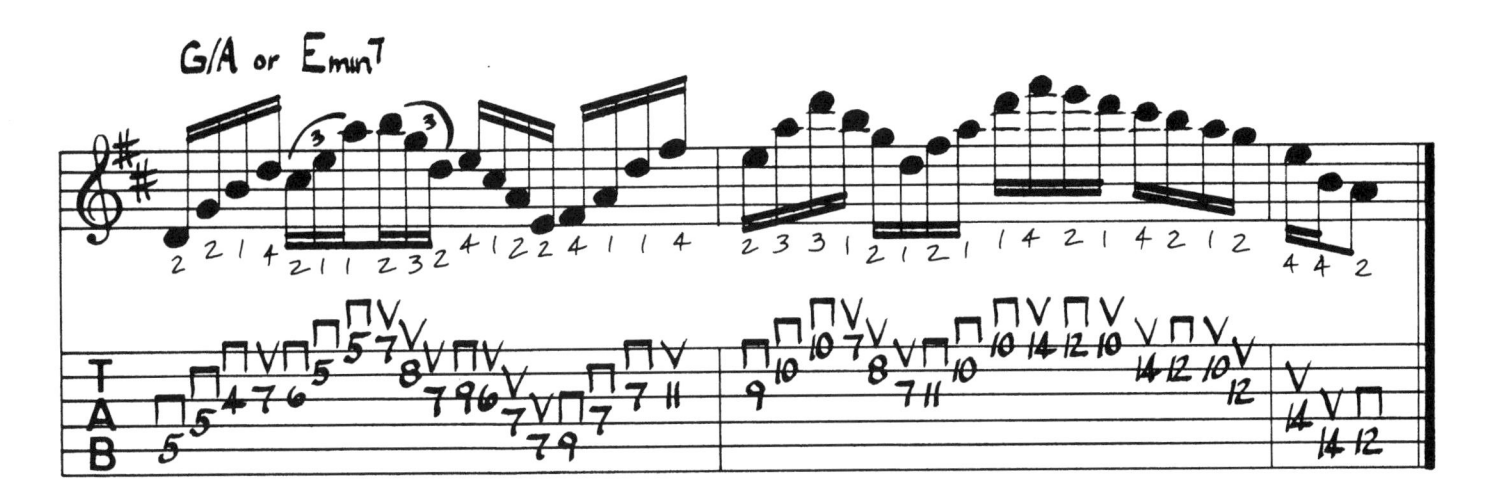

Lick #15   Cm7

Lick #16   Fmaj7

Techno-Rocker Flashmaster

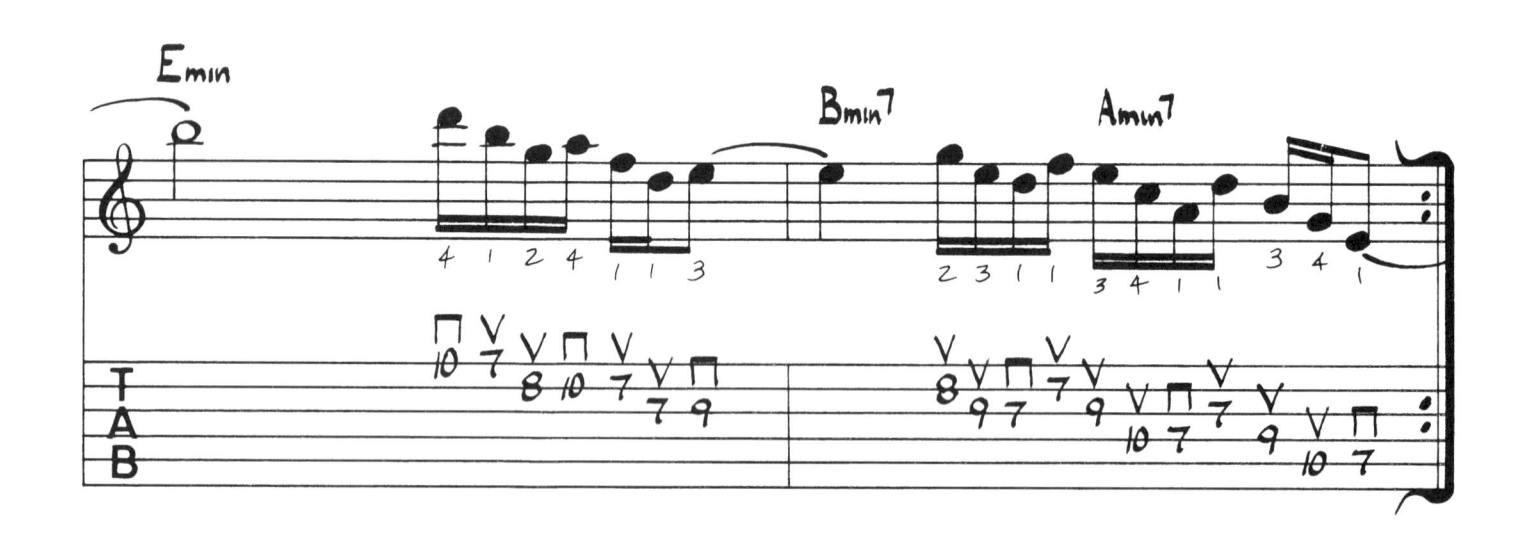

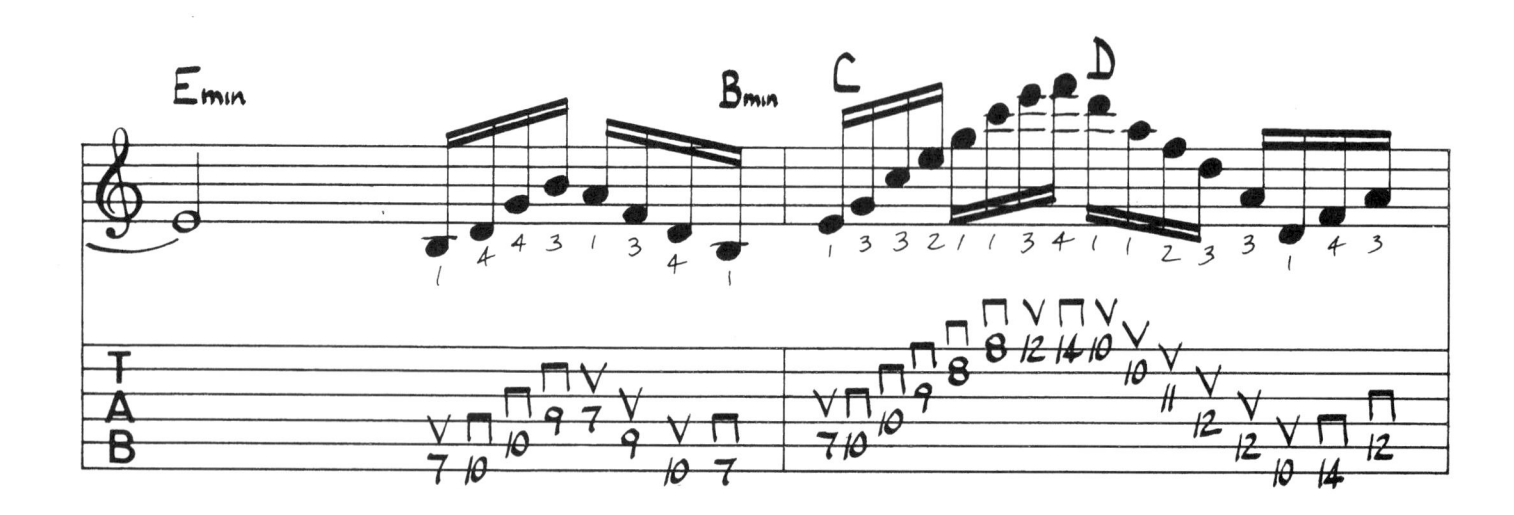

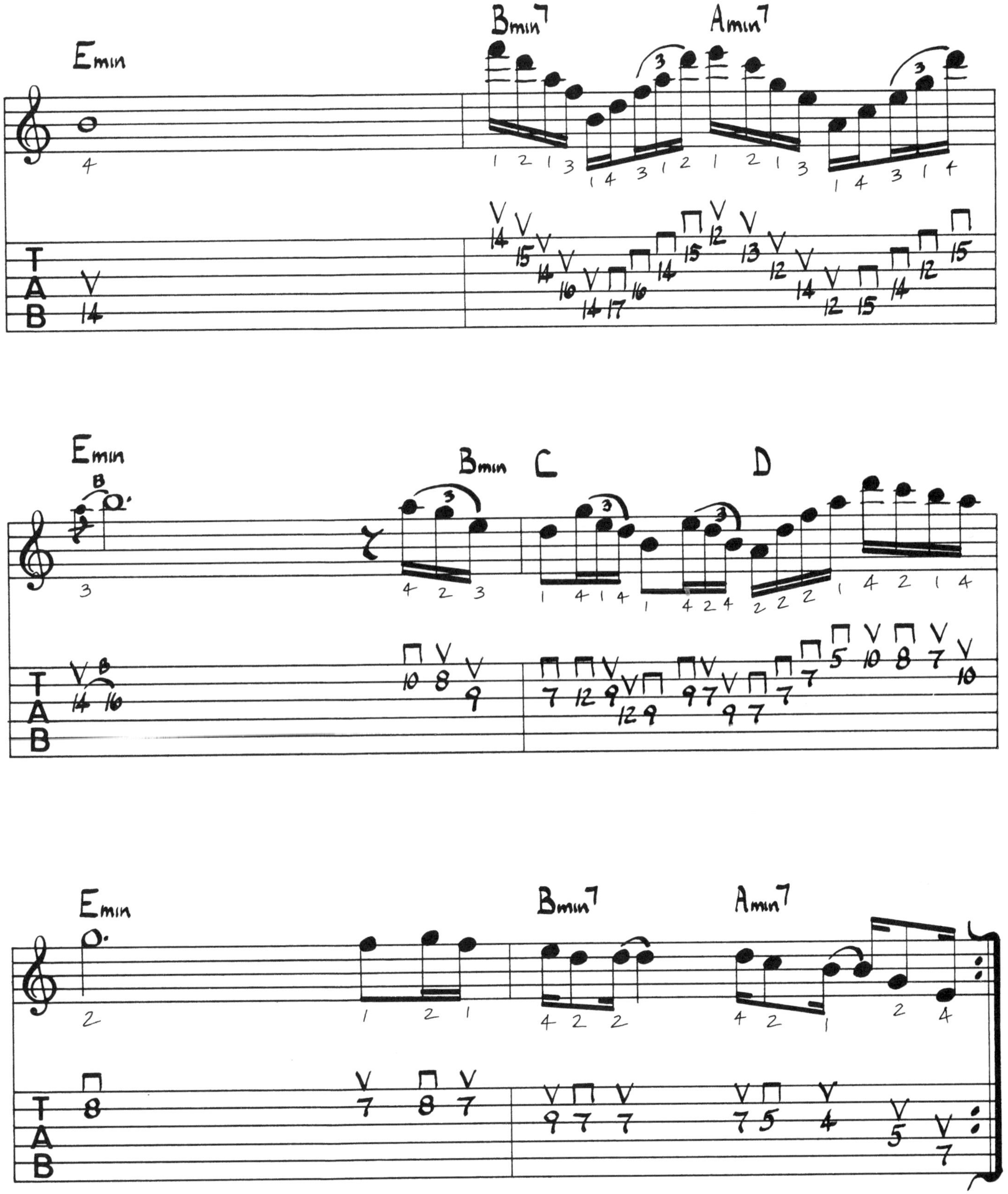
Emin
Bmin7
Amin7
Emin
Bmin
C
D
Emin
Bmin7
Amin7

Late Night

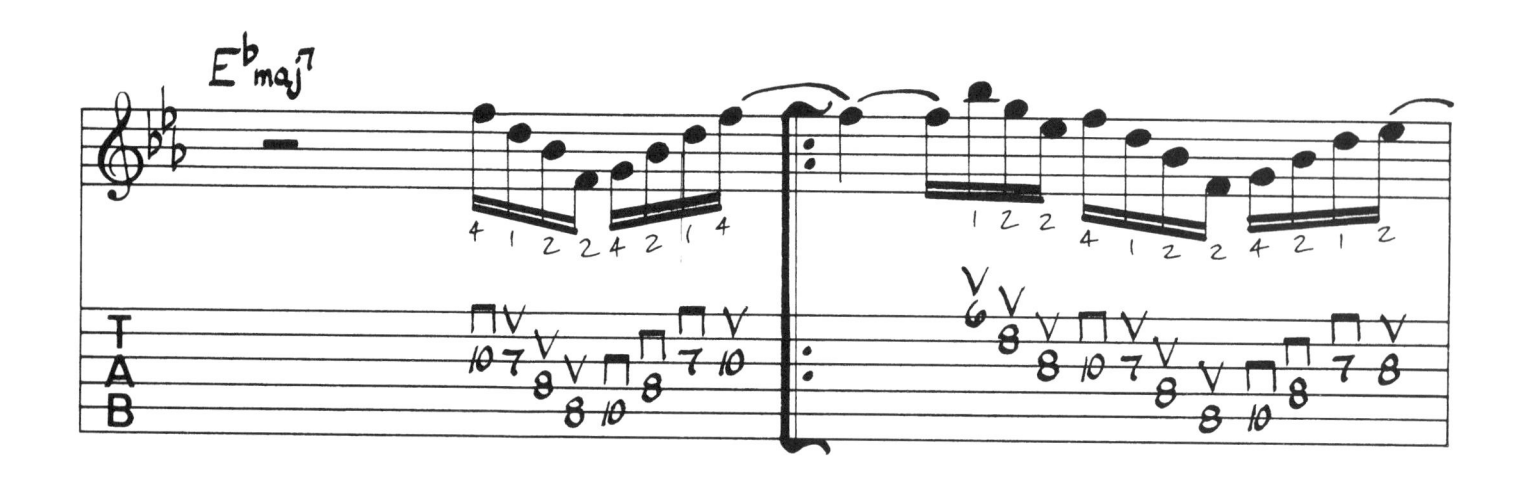

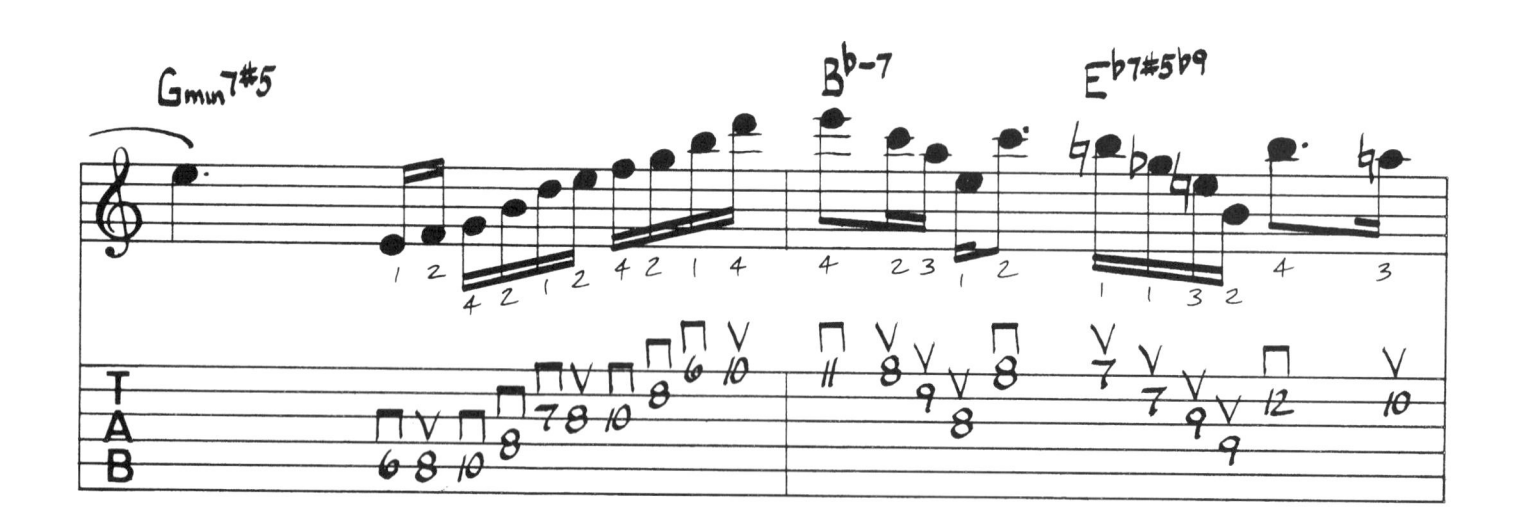

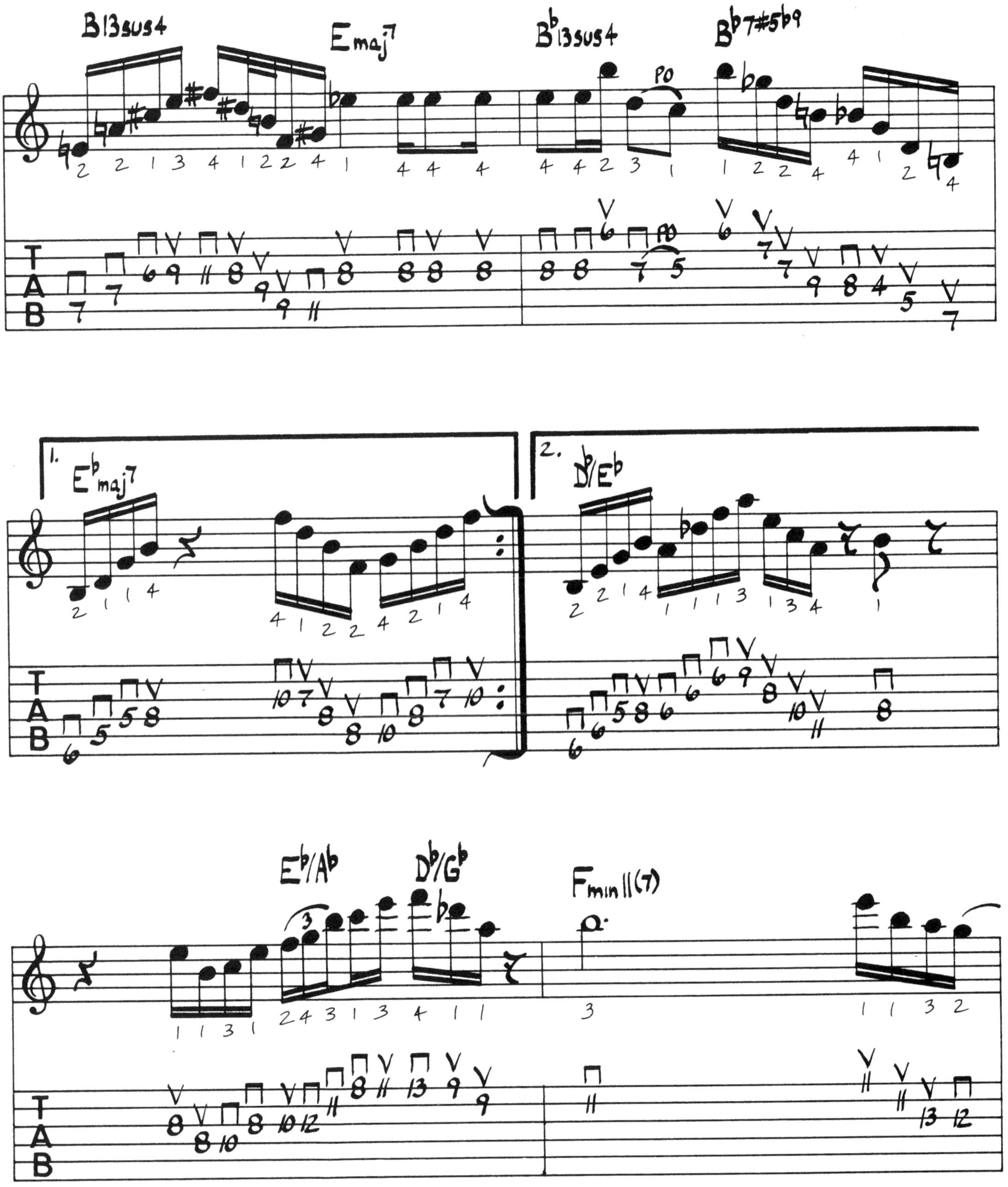
B13sus4
Emaj7
B♭13sus4
B♭7#5♭9
PO
E♭maj7
D♭/E♭
E♭/A♭
D♭/G♭
Fmin11(7)

Late Night (cont'd)

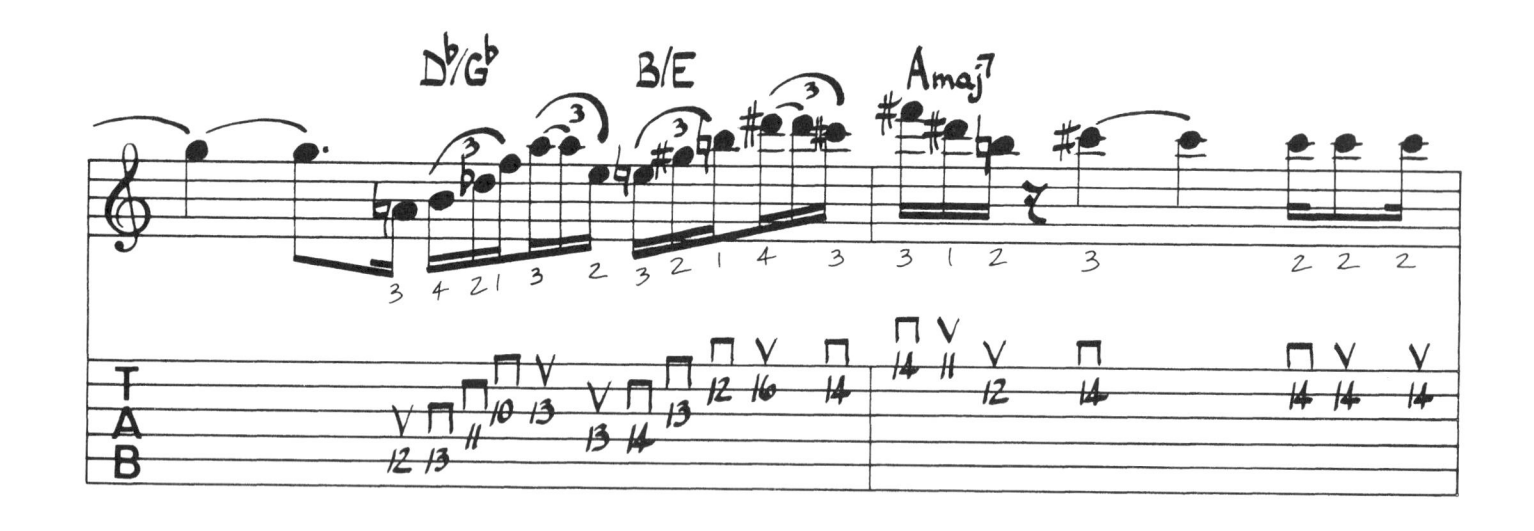

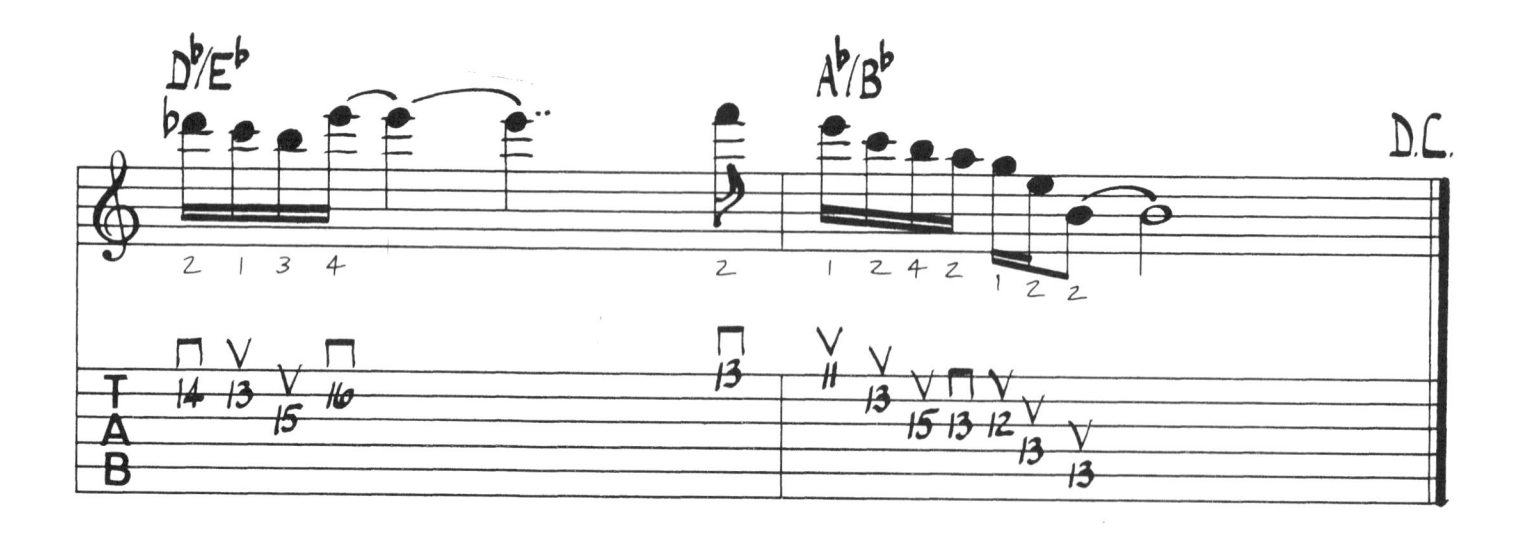

Note from the Author

Well fellow guitarists, that's about it! I know there are exercises in this book that will be difficult to play, but I know from my teaching experience at G.I.T. (Guitar Institute of Technology) that they are indeed possible to play with practice. Besides, there is a certain ecstacy one feels when conquering a difficult piece of music. I fully intended the book to present challenges otherwise there would be no benefit to you. Just remember that this is a new approach to guitar playing so be patient. I feel sure that you will obtain lots of useful information from these pages and help break down some barriers between you and the guitar and make you what you ultimately want to be, a MONSTER SPEED GUITARIST. Good luck to you!

Frank Gambale

Frank Gambale arrived in the U.S. in September 1982, an Italian Australian, to study at the renowned Guitar Institute of Technology (GIT) in Hollywood. Graduating with the highest honor, *Student of the Year Award*, he was offered a teaching position which he held for three years while performing in Los Angeles with his own band.

Frank's list of performance credits is long and varied, including such musicians as Chick Corea and the Elektric Band, with whom he won a Grammy and two nominations, Jean Luc Ponty, and Steve Smith and Vital Information.

In addition, Frank has two guitar models with the Ibanez company, and endorsements with many companies including D'Addario Strings, and DiMarzio pickups.

SELECTED DISCOGRAPHY

Passages
    (JVC)

The Great Explorers
    (JVC 2020)

Note Worker
    (JVC VICJ 75)

Thunder From Down Under
    (JVC 3321)

Frank Gambale "LIVE"
    (Legato/Important 1003)

A Present For the Future
    (Legato/Important 1002)

Brave New Guitar
    (Legato/Important 1001)

WITH VITAL INFORMATION

Easier Done Than Said

OTHERS

MVP - Truth In Shredding
    (Alan Holdsworth)